HOW TO TALK

CAN LEARN ABOUT

ANTI-RACISM AND

SOCIAL JUSTICE

Disclaimer Notice

Please note the information contained within this document is for education only. All efforts have been executed to present accurate, reliable, and up to date information. No warranties of any kind are implied. The contents from this book are derived from various sources. Please consult a licensed professional before attempting any techniques contained herein.

By reading this document, the reader agrees that under no circumstances are we responsible for any losses, direct or indirect, which are incurred as a result of the use of the information contained within this document, including, but not limited to, errors, omissions, or inaccuracies.

Preface

This book is dedicated to all the children out there, including my two very young kids, Thomas and Danilo. This book is also dedicated to all the very normal people that everyday still facing and resisting latent and institutionalized forms of racism, injustice, violence and ultimately unfair limitations to a fulfilling and enjoyable life.

The attempt is to give to the careers of these children a superficial knowledge about historical facts and figures and some awareness about important psychological developmental stages that take place in the life of each one of us. This is done to shade some light on how little people can easily pick up on everyday life information around them and build either a positive Self-awareness or a negative one. Without going too much into academic details and intricacies, the hope is to equip more adult careers possible with some knowledge and understanding about these processes and be able to act on them if necessary. Correct emerging negative concepts and ideas about one's Self and/or others, can help little people to flourish into emphatic, fair, responsible and caring people that the world is so needed of.

The bulk of the book focuses on the very concept of Racism, Anti-Racism and Social Justice so that careers know what they refer to and how to explain them. This is also important so that careers are able to introduce these concepts to their little people when needed. Following the idea that we lead by examples, it also provides some tips and tricks on how to be anti-racist, and how to behave if we are witness of or confronted with a racist incident.

Believing that there is only 'one-man race' and, in order to move beyond the effects that racism has on our mind and behavior, this book suggests to embrace a more nuanced and flexible concept of Ethnicity rather than 'Race'. This is done with the intention of overcoming prejudiced discriminations while still honoring our undisputable differences.

Introduction

What happens when racism normalizes and is part of the institutions themselves? With a smile and without being aware that they are racist, people will adopt it as a way of life, as part of their values and culture.

The film Green Book shows us the most normalized face of racism in the 60s in the United States. No one questioned why blacks should stay in different hotels, why they could not use the same bathroom as white, or why they could not go to certain restaurants.

What if the black in question is important? What if it has more power than any of the targets around it? Then, with a cheerful and friendly smile, you will be invited to demonstrate your skills and, when the time comes, you will be kindly separated. Because a black man will never be a target and, if he gets close, he must constantly demonstrate his talent. Don Shirley is paid to play in salons of wealthy, educated, and exquisite people, able to admire their talent, but it is better not to try to mix with them beyond the exhibition.

The hypocrisy of the most educated, of those who say they embrace the differences but know that there is a limit that they can never cross. Those wise people who criticize racism, machismo, or homophobia, but who are also elitists and will not let their elite falter. And they will do it unconsciously because it is taken as something normal and completely harmless. The high culture, unfortunately, has always been somewhat elitist. And that elitism is spread to Don Shirley in his eagerness to overcome, not to be a black anymore; although, deep down, he is aware of his reality. On the other hand, Tony Lip, with his dubious morals, does not fit that elite despite being white. He also bears his label, that of Italian American, the descendant of immigrants and, consequently, of the working class. Despite his apparent lack of culture, he can also enjoy music and even good words.

All this speech is reflected in Green Book and, at the same time, we can transfer it to our reality. Indeed, this segregation is no longer suffered in our day in the same way, but the traces of institutionalized racism are not easily erased. Let's think, for a moment, in our universities, is there diversity? Surely, very little. We do not live in the United States of the 60s, but we still live in a world that is excluded by origin, gender, sexual orientation, etc.

Green Book does not put its finger on the sore, it does not show us the crudest image of racism, but the most normalized, silent, and, perhaps, the most dangerous. Therefore, although it gives us nothing new, it conveys a message that, unfortunately, is timeless. It is no longer the "no to racism," it is the no to discrimination of whatever kind.

Whether or not Oscar deserved for the best film is another matter. Nor can we affirm that it is an essential and necessary film, but it achieves its purpose: it transmits us that good roll that it intends and will get us more than a smile.

Racism is the belief that a particular race is superior or lower than another, and that a person's social and moral characteristics are predetermined by their innate biological properties. Racial discrimination is the belief that different races should remain separate and separate from each other, mostly based on racism.

Racism has existed throughout human history. It can be defined as the belief that another person is less than a human because of one's hatred for someone else or any factor that is expected to reveal their skin color, language, traditions, birthplace, or basic nature of that person. Their wars affected slavery, nation-building, and legal codes.

Chapter 1 Making Sense of the World

Between 1525 and 1866, 12.5 million people were kidnapped from Africa and sent to the Americas through the transatlantic slave trade. Upon reaching the New World, some 3.9 million of the 10.7 million who survived the harrowing two-month journey were enslaved in the United States. Comprehending the sheer scale of this forced migration—and slavery's subse☐uent spread across the country via interregional trade—can be a daunting task, but as historian Leslie Harris told Smithsonian's Amy Crawford earlier this year, framing "these big concepts in terms of individual lives … can [help you] better understand what these things mean".

Take, for instance, the story of John Casor. Originally an indentured servant of African descent, Casor lost a 1654 or 1655 court case convened to determine whether his contract had lapsed. He became the first individual declared a slave for life in the United States. Manuel Vidau, a Yoruba man who was captured and sold to traders some 200 years after Casor's enslavement, later shared an account of his life with the British and Foreign Anti-Slavery Society, which documented his remarkable story—after a decade of enslavement in Cuba, he purchased a share in a lottery ticket and won enough money to buy his freedom—in records now available on the digital database "Freedom Narratives." (A separate, similarly document-based online resource emphasizes individuals described in fugitive slave ads, which historian Joshua Rothman describes as "sort of a little biography" providing insights on their subjects' appearance and attire.)

Finally, consider the life of Matilda McCrear, the last known survivor of the transatlantic slave trade. Kidnapped from West Africa and brought to the U.S. on the Clotilda, she arrived in Mobile, Alabama, in July 1860—more than 50 years after Congress had outlawed the import of enslaved labor. McCrear, who died in 1940 at the age of 81 or 82, "displayed a determined, even defiant streak" in her later life, wrote Brigit Katz earlier this year. She refused to use her former owner's last name, wore her hair in traditional Yoruba style and had a decades-long relationship with a white German man.

How American society remembers and teaches the horrors of slavery is crucial. But as recent studies have shown, many textbooks offer a sanitized view of this history, focusing solely on "positive" stories about black leaders like Harriet Tubman and Frederick Douglass. Prior to 2018, Texas schools even taught that states' rights and sectionalism—not slavery—were the main causes of the Civil War. And, in Confederate memorials across the country, historian Kevin M. Levin writes, enslaved individuals are often falsely portrayed as loyal slaves.

Accurately representing slavery might require an updated vocabulary, argued historian Michael Landis in 2015: Outdated "[t]erms like 'compromise' or 'plantation' served either to reassure worried Americans in a Cold War world, or uphold a white supremacist, sexist interpretation of the past." Rather than referring to the Compromise of 1850, call it the Appeasement of 1850—a term that better describes "the uneven nature of the agreement," according to Landis. Smithsonian scholar Christopher Wilson wrote, too, that widespread framing of the Civil War as a battle between equal entities lends legitimacy to the Confederacy, which was not a nation in its own right, but an "illegitimate rebellion and unrecognized political entity." A 2018 Smithsonian magazine investigation found that the literal costs of the Confederacy are immense: In the decade prior, American taxpayers contributed

$40 million to the maintenance of Confederate monuments and heritage organizations.

To better understand the immense brutality ingrained in enslaved individuals' everyday lives, read up on Louisiana's Whitney Plantation Museum, which acts as "part reminder of the scars of institutional bondage, part mausoleum for dozens of enslaved people who worked (and died) in [its] sugar fields, … [and] monument to the terror of slavery," as Jared Keller observed in 2016. Visitors begin their tour in a historic church populated by clay sculptures of children who died on the plantation's grounds, then move on to a series of granite slabs engraved with hundreds of enslaved African Americans' names. Scattered throughout the experience are stories of the violence inflicted by overseers.

The Whitney Plantation Museum is at the forefront of a vanguard of historical sites working to confront their racist pasts. In recent years, exhibitions, oral history projects and other initiatives have highlighted the enslaved people whose labor powered such landmarks as Mount Vernon, the White House and Monticello. At the same time, historians are increasingly calling attention to major historical figures' own slave-holding legacies: From Thomas Jefferson to George Washington, William Clark of Lewis and Clark, Francis Scott Key, and other Founding Fathers, many American icons were complicit in upholding the institution of slavery. Washington, Jefferson, James Madison and Aaron Burr, among others, sexually abused enslaved females working in their households and had often-overlooked biracial families.

Though Abraham Lincoln issued the Emancipation Proclamation on January 1, 1863, the decree took two-and-a-half years to fully enact. June 19, 1865—the day Union Gen. Gordon Granger informed the enslaved individuals of Galveston, Texas, that they were officially free—is now known as Juneteenth: America's "second independence day," according to NMAAHC. Initially celebrated mainly in Texas, Juneteenth spread across the country as African Americans fled the South in what is now called the Great Migration.

At the onset of that mass movement in 1916, 90 percent of African Americans still lived in the South, where they were "held captive by the virtual slavery of sharecropping and debt peonage and isolated from the rest of the country," as Isabel Wilkerson wrote in 2016. (Sharecropping, a system in which formerly enslaved people became tenant farmers and lived in "converted" slave cabins, was the impetus for the 1919 Elaine Massacre, which found white soldiers collaborating with local vigilantes to kill at least 200 sharecroppers who dared to criticize their low wages.) By the time the Great Migration—famously chronicled by artist Jacob Lawrence—ended in the 1970s, 47 percent of African Americans called the northern and western United States home.

Conditions outside the Deep South were more favorable than those within the region, but the "hostility and hierarchies that fed the Southern caste system" remained major obstacles for black migrants in all areas of the country, according to Wilkerson. Low-paying jobs, redlining, restrictive housing covenants and rampant discrimination limited opportunities, creating inequality that would eventually give rise to the civil rights movement.

"The Great Migration was the first big step that the nation's servant class ever took without asking," Wilkerson explained. " ... It was about agency for a people who had been denied it, who had geography as the only tool at their disposal. It was an expression of faith, despite the terrors they had

[18]

survived, that the country whose wealth had been created by their ancestors' unpaid labor might do right by them."

Black Americans revolution

On June 17, 2015, nine people were killed in a black church in Charleston, South Carolina. The murderer is a white racist young man, 21, who is a supporter of white domination, those who long for apartheid. This massacre comes after a series of police murders stating that the persecution of blacks had not ended in the United States. Michael Brown, 18, was killed in Ferguson by a policeman who did not see the judiciary as a necessity to stand trial. Eric Garner, 44, was strangled in New York by a policeman who was not brought to trial. John Crawford, 22, was killed by a policeman at a supermarket in Ohio while playing a game, and the authorities have seen no need to prosecute him. Tamer Rice, 12, was killed by a policeman in Cleveland while he was playing with a toy weapon. Walter Scott, 50, was killed by eight bullets in the back by a policeman in South Carolina. Freddy Gray, 25, was treated cruelly to death by six policemen in Baltimore after they broke his spine.

The list is long. At the heart of the First World Power, and in my country, it prides itself on being the habitat of freedom, the police, or their representatives, kill hundreds of people every year - and nobody knows exactly how many. A British newspaper has counted 500 cases since January 2015 - and a high rate of them are black, all without accountability most of the time. It was in similar circumstances that, in 1964, the situation in the Harlem ghetto exploded, after a black youth was killed by a policeman. This was followed by a series of unrest that accompanied the outbreak of the black uprising. This gift came after ten years of continuous struggle for civil rights, followed by years of unrest and various movements. During this period, all laws of apartheid agreeing to civil rights were repealed, and racial discrimination began to be reviewed. That is 1970, after two decades of struggle, African Americans managed to join the police in the major cities, and some of them became mayors, sheriffs, and even congressmen or army officers. In 2008, we elect a black person for the presidency of the United States, Barack Obama. Isn't that as some interested people indicate - the best proof that the United States has eliminated the persecution of blacks? What we see today is that discrimination still applies in America, as well as racial discrimination and even racism itself.

Modern Era Movements & Leaders

Black Lives Matter

In response to the acquittal of George Zimmerman for the murder of Trayvon Martin and the dehumanization of Martin by the media, Alicia Garza, Patrisse Cullors, and Opal Tometi created the hashtag and call-to-action #BlackLivesMatter. The focus of the movement is to affirm the vibrant contributions of Black people to American culture, to reaffirm the humanity of Black Americans, and to organize and affect change by revitalizing the Black Liberation Movement and fight against

[21]

the systemic oppression, racism, and murder of Black people in the United States. It is important to note that while the original movement began online, Black Lives Matter, as an official organization and the team lead by Alicia, Patrisse, and Opal, has become a physical movement that organizes events and actions.

Bree Newsome, Activist

A few weeks after the tragic murders of nine people at Emanuel African Methodist Episcopal church, Bree Newsome, a thirty-year-old activist, filmmaker, and artist, scaled the thirty-foot flagpole outside the South Carolina statehouse and removed a symbol of racism, hate, and oppression: the Confederate flag.

While the police arrested Newsome, her actions helped spark a conversation about systemic racism and the removal of all symbols that honor the Confederacy. Many White people in the South believe that the flag is representative of American history, but for Black people, the flag symbolizes a South so invested in the system of slavery that they would rather secede from the Union than dismantle the institution. With the flag and monuments honoring Confederate soldiers decorating public spaces and in government buildings, Black people are reminded that this country is not a safe space for those with brown skin.

"The Lord is my light and my salvation, whom
shall I fear?"
Quote from the Bible

Tarana Burke

In the year 2006, Tarana Burke raised awareness about sexual abuse and sexual harassment by using the phrases "Me Too" on Twitter. She is an American Civil Rights activist. The phrase she wished to say to other victims of sexual abuse to tell them they are not alone. She created JustBeInc.com to promote mental and physical wellness among women that are marginalized.

The goal of "Me Too" is to help young women of color from low-wealth communities heal from sexual assault through empathy and by providing resources to help facilitate their healing. The "me too" movement became well known when famous actresses, such as Gwyneth Paltrow and Uma Thurman among others, began sharing their experiences in Hollywood, the focus of the movement has and continues to be on (BIPOC) Black, Indigenous, and People of Color who are often more likely to endure sexual assault.

Tarana Burke was named by Time Magazine in 2017 as "Person of the Year" along with others. She continues to help bring opportunity for young BIPOC to conquer the difficulty that they deal with as the Senior Director of (GGE) Girls for Gender Equality (GGE) in Brooklyn, New York. She also confers issues of poverty, sexism, transphobia, racial injustices, harassment, and homophobia through GGE.

Chapter 2 Who am I?

This chapter is going to move away from the historical facts and figures of black Americans to move toward an understanding on how the formation of identity for every human being is a necessary path. Each one of us, particularly during some critical developmental stages, such as adolescence, will try to synthesize different parts of our being and try to find a place in the world. The aim is to shade some light on when and how children at very early stages start this process of identity formation. So, as parents, if we are aware that these processes are happening in the life of our children, we could act in order to facilitate a healthy identity seeking process.

Erik Erikson's Perspective of Identity

One of the most renewed theory about identity formation was conceptualized in the second half of the 20th century by sociopsychologist Erik Erikson. He was a student of Anna Freud, the daughter of the world renewed psychoanalyst Sigmund Freud. This is why most of Erikson's early theories are strongly influenced by Freud's work. Erikson formulates that the Ego, this individual center of organized experience and reasonable planning is, on the one hand, threatened from the anarchy of the desires and on the other hand, is threatened from the restrictions of the group(s) of belonging (Erikson, 1975: 959). The ego, in the early Freudian sense, stands in conflict with the biological steered subconscious desires, called identity, and the realm beyond the family or the larger sociological group (the super-ego).

Following Freud, Erikson reasons that the super-ego, as a moral corrective of this virtually encircled ego, is the internalization of all restrictions to which ego must subjugate itself (Freud 1914). The development of these restrictions by the takeover of social norms and values of negative connotations by influencing control on the part of the family leads to a decoupling of the ego from the rest of the society– the world "outside" - qua family-oriented projection.

The development of the personal identity, the ego-synthesis, is based on the perception of the child, that his way to process experiences is a successful variant of the group identity, and stands in harmony with the space-time-concept and the life plan of the group. Furthermore, the ego-synthesis is based on the statement of recognition of this equality and continuity also by other group members. On the terminal point of the ego-synthesis, which is partitioned into different segments, stands the adolescence which shows great differences concerning duration, intensity, and ritualization in different societies.

Erikson makes a distinction for a moral categorization between "positive" and "negative" group identity which is characterized by certain ideologies. The orientation need for the adolescent is canalized by the integration in the ideology determining the group identity. For Erikson, an ideological system is a thing closed in itself by common symbols, ideas, and ideals, (whether it's been based on an explicit dogma, a hidden world view, a highly structured world view, a political about the opinion or a "way of life") which gives his followers together one, even if systematically simplistic orientation in space and time, mean and aim. Group identity perpetuates therefore ideology and vice versa. The next higher step of the identification of the 'individual, the solidarity, holds together the normal identities. Prejudices compared with other groups manifest themselves in the unaware negative identity being a part of the ego-identity. A necessary component of every group formation is the unaware association of national and ethnic identity with moral and sexual alternatives. Traditional group identities and solidarities have been formed on agrarian, feudal, patrician, or mercantile ideologies. These have been corrupted by the technical and business development of modern times, nevertheless, they still very valuable.

The identification of a single person with the ideology of his group leads to the function of relevance groups, which Erikson recognizes to be integrative. Accordingly, ideological and identity-establishing groups are of economic, ethnic, and religious nature. The lack of positive identity finding in the mentioned groups, resultant from social border situations, leads to an evil turn to a negative group identity. Then the young people search for negative group identities in forming spontaneous cliques which lead from building neighborhood-gangs and jazz-bands up to narcotic-consumers and criminal-groupings. The avoidance of such-like social border situations is necessary therefore for the development of a positive individual identity and can be achieved under the instructions and guidance of ideological leading figures which create new solidarities and identifications.

Answering to the question on how the masses which followed the revolutionary elite had to become ideologically integrated, Erikson said: "The ideological avant-garde of the pioneers of the Israeli Kibbutzim as well as the American colonists, which used also a historical moratorium which offered the discovery of an empty continent to them created a new life form" (ibid.: 207; emphases by the author). The existence of a historical moratorium by the discovery of an empty continent is obviously incorrect for American as well as for Palestine history, moreover ignorant, there was neither a moratorium nor an empty continent. Despite that Erikson

[31]

comes to the result, that positive group consciousness and with it also identity can be initiated by ideological elites and has to be done in this way.

The consciousness of all affiliations to social groups which originates from reflexive processes and role takeovers can become behavior steering initiative. In general, six categories of social identity can be stated: "social statuses, group's membership, "labels", derived statuses, types and personal identity" (Rosenberg 1979).

The personal identity is limited in contrast to the prementioned, socially founded aspects, to the specific individual attributes. For example, physical or intellectual qualities, psychological characteristic features, personal taste, sympathies or antipathies, etc. which own great social relevance concerning the development and conversion of settings and behavior at a general social level beyond the narrower personal relation circle.

Erikson´s merit is absolute. To have reconducted the prevailing source of the meaning of identity to the socialization process in the family and other immediate meaningful groups. This closed familiar compound is, of course, only one part of the identity development influenced also by the "outside world". In contrast to Freud, he puts the Self, the Ego, into the center of his investigations and admits that the areas of Self-confidence and Self-evaluation has even a bigger space (Goethals/Strauss 1991: 3) that goes beyond the immediate circle of meaningful groups to include the society at large where that individual is brought up . Erikson's concept of identity finding develops in the type of the competitive male representative of the American society, whose attributes are activity and striving for autonomy, linked with patriotic pride in its nation and its achieving consciousness (Stross in 1991: 91, the emphasis is mine). The inclusion of ethnic minorities in a "new identity to be developed" is oriented in the values and norms of the US-American middle class and presupposes their takeover for the development of a "healthy personality". The blacks, men and women have a common experience: they have been the "different ones", while the adult white man has been ´the normal´ (Erikson 1975:130). Deviant behavior and existing contradictions in one's person are founded in the lacking willingness to identify with these positive values. Nevertheless, mechanisms of the group-evolution remain extensively ignored. Relevant groups beyond the family for the finding of identity and integration remain blurred outlined; this lies naturally also in the topic of Erikson´s attempt about the creation of individual identity reasonably. However, Erikson´s identity idea is not accepted undivided on account of its relative variations (Haußer 1983).

The Perception of the Self-Concept

The possible perceptions of the self-concept are, like those of the identity, different and complex and are treated here therefore from the scientific point of view and they are a central theme in this work. The concept of the "self" is called, due to various disciplines, also "ego", "Proprium" or "identity"; the herewith related contents are also manifold. The main focus of the investigation in social science lies in the functions of language and social interaction as a basis of the self-concept. Within social psychology, the main attention lies in cognitive and motivational aspects, for example, of the action motivation. The self-concept plays an important role in the theory-construction of ethnicity and, hence, should be explained in its main features.

The idea of the self-concept results from the ability of reflexive thinking, regarding itself as a subject as well as an

[34]

object, to step with itself virtually into a dialogue. The different aspects of the self-concept can be split into two coarse categories: Identities and self-valuations. These are structured into certain sub-groups with differentiated shapes. Identity can appear as a social or personal identity actively or passively. Self-evaluations correspond to situate specific identities or reflect the continuity more fundamentally of long-term self-views. In general can be said, that the self-concept:

- allows judgments about the person and their decisions and determinates them substantially;
- is available and retrievable in principle (close to behavior);
- delivers a basis for the prediction of one's behavior;
- Makes the person resistant against the admission of such information which does not fit in the pattern (Sader in 1980).

Ethnicity

Andre Gingrich picks out as a central theme the concept of "ethnicity" in seven theses: which can be derived from the before treated theoretical attempts:

- Ethnicity calls the respective relation between two or several groups that differ culturally from each other in important ways, like appearance, believes, customs etc.

- As well as every person that tends to be egocentric, ethnic groups also tend under certain circumstances to be ethnocentric. Under threats Ethnocentrism is sometimes inevitable, but it is seldom right.

- Ethnicity is no just linguistic, or wearing certain dress for "racial" or "national" reasons. Ethnic differences can easily lead to racism but to ignore ethnic differences, however, it also quite dangerous.

- Ethnicity and nationality are not identical. Nations are political communities which live or want to live permanently in the same state association. However, ethnicity often crosses national and state borders.

- Ethnicity is not identical to culture either. Ethnicity as a relational network actualizes only certain aspects of the involved cultures in this interrelation and combines these with external effects.

- Ethnicity changes in the course of the time over and over again. As well as it is now, it does not remain.

- Ethnicity varies according to the circumstances. As well as it is here, it is not everywhere, otherwise.

The concept of ethnicity is underlying a steadily continuing discourse that is steered by the varying real circumstances in the sphere of the acting and affected persons. It can always go in new directions and demonstrates availability and attempts to be modifiable or adaptable to new circumstances.

Chapter 3 Psychological Understanding of Prejudice

The main driver of prejudice is contempt and hostility against the minority/ies. These sentiments are established on feelings of predominance by the dominant part. There are still areas in the United States, for instance, where white individuals exclude and left behind other minorities from community activities and initiatives. Even when minority groups have organizations there, work there, however they can't live in the area permanently or be part of the local community because considered inferior. This is a form of prejudice.

Control the Mind Control the Person

Concerning the brain science of prejudice, mind control is at stake here. Psyche control is otherwise called mind-clearing or coercive influence includes instilling individuals to the degree that their chance of thinking is weakened. The taught individual cannot wonder why they do what they do. Without a doubt, when you control an individual's psyche, you have them in your hold and they will do your offering.

How Brainwashing Has Been Used to Control the Mind.

Brainwashing is a type of psychological control that directs an individual's capacity to settle on decisions without being forced or pressured. When an individual has been indoctrinated, they lose the capacity to break down information and make reasoning without caring what others let them know. In the brain research of bigotry, biased people have been programmed to imagine that they are unrivaled and a few of us are here to be seen and their claims be heard, but not others. Sometime people can be persuaded that other are useless, particularly when they belong to other ethnic groups.

Racism and Denying Yourself Worth It

We need to confront a few realities here. Bigotry involves looking into the prevalence of an individual or group over the inadequacy of another. This isn't a dominant game. One group can utilize discourse on the apparent mediocrity of the minority to show their predominance. The blame becomes both the jury and the adjudicator - what a bent world! At whatever point bigotry is presented, you can be certain somebody will lose - and it's consistently the minority.

Inferiority Complex and Racism

In America, bigotry is normal and comes in different structures and shapes including police ruthlessness and racial profiling among others. This has brought about low confidence among the minorities particularly of dark skin color. As a matter of fact, low confidence is the main purpose behind inclusion in lawful offenses. Why? Since bigotry is about dominant force and when one individual is denied their intellectual capacity, they will respond to show their disappointment.

Superiority Complex Psychology

It is both absurd and ludicrous to realize that the prevalence complex is a type of guard system which individuals utilize to reward for the substandard complex. Such individuals accept that their worth is relied upon belittling and harming others.

Assassinating a Person's Character with Racism

The brain science of prejudice includes character death. Character death can be portrayed as a planned and steady procedure that expects to insult or abuse the validity of an individual or gathering of individuals. Individuals who kill others' characters utilize different strategies including misdirecting data, demeaning, slander and control. This may prompt dismissal by other people who may not have the foggiest idea about the genuine truth - does this ring a bell? Prejudice is incredible and will frequently retaliate through character death.

Nothing is permanent here though. On the off chance that today we are living in very much assembled houses and not caverns, if today we are utilizing current ovens and not kindling, if today we are strolling completely dressed and not exposed, nothing is unimaginable. At some point - bigotry will be history.

How Children on Different Stages Might Interpret and Be Affected

One of the most famous and significant study on children cognitive development was developed by the French psychologist Jean Piaget. The approach was first available in 1952 and continued many years after through extensive children observation. Even though Piaget was fascinated with the way children responded to their surroundings, he suggested a more influential position for them than that proposed by the learning theory. Piaget approach is based on the assumption that the knowledge of a child is made of schemas.

Schemas are persistently customized by two similar processes, which Piaget referred to as accommodation and assimilation. Assimilation is the progression of taking in novel data by integrating it into a subsisting schema. For instance, the general public assimilates novel experiences by recounting them to the preexisting knowledge of things. Conversely, accommodation is described as what takes place at the time the schema changes to contain new knowledge. According to the French psychologist, cognitive development entails a continuing effort to attain a balance flanked by accommodation and assimilation, which he referred to as equilibration.

Jean Piaget developed a cognitive development theory, which described as well as explained the transformation of children as well as adolescents' logical thinking. He identified several cognitive development stages that all learners have to go through. Generally, consistent with Piaget's cognitive development theory, the child experiences diverse developmental stages:

- the sensorimotor stage (0 to 2 years)
- the preoperational (2 to7)
- the concrete operational (7 to 12)
- the formal-operational stage (12 to15)

The first stage is the sensorimotor stage or just infancy. In most cases, these children will not be affected, for example, by television program. Ideally, this period has six sub-stages; intelligence remains established via motor activity without symbolic use. The world's knowledge is limited, except developing because it is founded on physical experiences and interactions. Children obtain object durability at about seven months (memory). Mobility (physical development) permits the child to start developing new intellectual aptitudes. Several symbolic (language) aptitudes are developed later of this stage.

The second stage is preoperational thinking. This takes place from approximately 2 to 3 to about seven years. Partly logical thought or deliberation starts at these years. The child reasons merely from one particular piece of information to one more and decide based in perceptual cues. However, preoperational thinking is capable of making basic sense of the world but, more often than not, remains illogical. Ideally, children in this period have complexity in accepting another individual's viewpoint. Piaget regarded them as egocentrism. However, children's thinking at this stage remains ego-centric and focuses on the instant look of things.

The concrete operational period is the third stage of Piaget's, from about 7 to 8 years to 12 to 14. This stage is connected to the direct exploration of objects. It entails states that need an understanding of concurrent changes in various features of objects. The child at this stage can discriminate his/her point of view from others as well as make assessments as well as reflects on communication. Also, he is capable of deducing meanings, infer incidents not presented, and "detect hidden meanings" (Greenfield 2019).

In summary, children between 7 and 11 demonstrate an excellent aptitude to handle what they see and experience. They are incredibly open and have a generally positive approach towards psychologically appealing sections. By 10 and 11, after a long period when the cognitive skills have grown significantly, children develop a somewhat more critical attitude. For example, most of the children after 10 and the adolescents tend not to limit themselves to children's animations but also follow popular adult series. This stage of life is quite important for the aim of this book. In fact, this developmental stage is important to consider when talking about how ideas and prejudice about others can be formed in the mind of young people through completely normal daily activities, such as, conversations during meal time in the family or watching television programs.

Piaget studies and observations, particularly of young children is of great relevance for the understanding of the possible roots of racial discrimination and how it can be understood and put into practices even by young children. According to Piaget, children actively construct their reality as the result of their ideas and their experiences. This observation was further develop in the 1940s, by psychologists Kenneth Bancroft Clark and his wife, Mamie Phipps Clark through the world-famous experiment of the black and white dolls. During this highly controversial but still relevant study, the spouses have managed to shade some light on how children as young as 6 perceived ideas of beauty and preference. During the experiment, only black children from segregated areas were observed. All of them were presented with black and white dolls and when asked which doll they liked best and preferred to play with, the great majority of them chose the white one. Although, this study is considerate definitely unethical and controversial today for the harm done to these children, it undeniably opened a wide door on the understanding of the creation of identity and, for the sake of this book, on the origin of prejudice, which then can feed in to racism.

Chapter 4 What is Racism?

Would we all agree that Racism is defined differently by different sources? Racism means different things to different individuals and different groups.

Definition(s):

- Discrimination, abuse, antagonism, unfair treatment, hate, or resentment of a group of human beings because of a system's perceived notions that they are inferior, by genetics and/or less valuable based on character and/or behavior.

- People's racial differences being the basis for separation and exclusion.
- Anti-Blackness.

The belief that people's qualities and characteristics are influenced by their race is it is not just a generalization, but it is actually a total lie. This kind of generalization seeks to dehumanize people and further creates separation among races. Although, there are certain existing qualities and characteristics that are influenced by people's genetics, as well as their culture, norms, and common interests, most often it is the social-economic relegation and class structure that determine the opportunities and chances that most people will get in life. For example, attending the best schools in the richest neighborhoods is been proven to be a determinant factor for not extremely bright children to have a successful career. But what if you are a very bright kid living in a deprived area attending the local school? Well, you can still succeed in life but you must endure much more through the social and economic difficulties you will find yourself in. And you must prove even more your talent.

A system of racism usually has a dominant side, which can be supported by institutions like Governments or just scattered self-interest groups throughout the national territory, whose objective is to enforce the idea of dominance through separatism, control, and the destruction physical and none of another race. Throughout history, we have seen endless dramatic events that were racially motivated; these shapes and mold our present perceptions of the human virtues and moral standing.

Beliefs are supporting the idea that we humans are civil, selfless beings with sprinklings of a few immoral and ruthless individuals. There is also the notion that most people cannot be trusted, "as we can see on the news every day that the overall human condition is soiled and spoiled by decadence, evil and immorality". Now, when it comes to the topic of race/racism, these perceptions are equally distributed among people. While some individuals believe racism is gone or has been significantly reduced compared to a certain time in the past, some members of society believe that large numbers of people are interested in the oppression and destruction of another race or races.

People lived in denial for years regarding racism, because denial puts them in a safe emotional place. People were in denial, so much that different races would be around each other with a tight uncomfortable tension and ignore it as if it's not there. There were awkward moments where each individual would be aware of the truth but behave clueless in each other's presence just appear civil. It's amazing how many people are in denial, yet these very people who exist in their minds. The very minds that think different degrees of racist and prejudice thoughts. Which means most people are out of touch with their minds and emotions.

In the past, laws were passed against the blatant discrimination and attacks on "minorities." Some laws were also removed to ensure freedom and integration between white people and black people. People subsequently spent years evaluating the policies of the past and also their behaviors and beliefs.

Eventually, people began to feel guilty and ashamed because their evaluations of the past made them seem inhumane and uncivilized by today's standards. People took time to reflect on their old ways and became somewhat more conscious of their behaviors and attitudes towards others. Think, for instance, the perception that German people have of their Nazi past.

Who are the real racists?

Most people today still identify themself with a 'race'. To what extend governmental or institutional racial profiling is influencing that is less and less debatable. Think, for instance, when you need to fill in most forms to enroll yourself or your children to a doctor surgery or to a school. However, more and more people today tend to talk about ethnicity/ies and intentionally avoid to talk about the more disadvantageous term 'race'. This is not just because talking about race can be detrimental but actually because they realize that there is one race the "one-man race." Ethnicity is a more nuanced term that encloses also a multiplicity of aspects (not just physical appearance) such as, historical past, costumes, believes etc.

However, most people today still identify themselves with a 'race'. And it is exactly this enormous pool of people that we need to understand and challenge in their assumptions in order to really wipe out racism from the face of earth and make it a thing of the past. Even the people who claim that they don't identify with a race, still do. To say "I don't identify with a

[53]

race", is to indirectly identify with a race. You are acknowledging that race exists by not identifying with one; this means, on some small level, you recognize your racial position in society, where you can identify or not identify with it. This is a form of indirect racial identification.

To say, "I don't see race," is to acknowledge that there is "race" to see, which means you see race. To say, "Race does not exist," is to confirm the concept of race, which means you believe that race exists.

When people say these things, it is not necessarily true for them. The intention may be good, but it is not actually what they truly believe. These are the things people want to believe or what they wish they could believe. These are things that people say because they believe it's right, but not because this where they are.

Being that we all, in some shape or form, identify with a race, we dissociate ("dis-identify") with other races. You cannot claim a group without separating yourself from the ones you don't identify with.

Once this identification process begins, you will inevitably form ideas, thoughts, and beliefs about the other groups, based on what makes them good or bad and different or the same as you. This is the pre-judging level of racism; in other words, this is how/where prejudice begins.

You will not be able to look at anything or anyone that you believe is separate or different from you, without processing some negative and positive things that you know about them.

To see someone and judge them as different or separate from you is the first level of prejudice. Bigger prejudice and racist thoughts and beliefs grow from this basis. WE ARE ALL PREJUDICED and WE ARE ALL RACIST. It is a self-perpetuating process that will never ends up until we stop talking about race. Recognize and accept 'one-man race' and start talking about ethnicities in order to acknowledge our actual differences is an obliged step, if not the only step, we have to overcome the self-perpetuating process of racism. Let's see it more in detail what racism does to us.

Who can be racist?

Some "pro-black" interest groups, defining racism as simply, "White Supremacy," suggesting that only those people who are either white, identify as white and/or benefit from white skin privilege, can be racist. They believe that people in the black community are not in the social/political position to be racist, as they suffered at the hands of white supremacy.

The people who are at the receiving end of racism, not only acquire resistance towards their haters, but also a disdain and rejection of the people in their groups. The resistance towards their haters is accepted because it is expected, due to the abuse suffered at the hands of the "haters" throughout history and the present day.

The disdain for their "own" people derives from their internalized feelings. This is when the hated starts to hate his reflection because it reminds him of why he is hated.

A strong need for mainstream acceptance sends him in the direction of adapting to the requirements of the mainstream ideals, after which he carries scorn for those in his race or community who have not confirmed. So not only are the "victims" capable of racism, but they harbor much more resentment because they send it in more than one direction. The process described can be referred to as Racism; even though it is more self-directed, it still pertains to the subject of race.

The people who support the idea that "Racism is White supremacy", believe that people of darker skin tones cannot be racist because they are at the victim end of racism, and they don't benefit from white supremacy, as it tends to loosely include even those who aren't European-Caucasian but possess whiter or lighter skin.

However, let's go deeper..

For hundreds of years (and possibly thousands), there has always been favor given to people of lighter complexions. The concept of white supremacy is rooted in the belief that people of whiter skin belong to or are coming from a superior lineage. The whiter, the better- and the closer you get to white in appearance, the more acceptance you will get by the majority of beings who benefit from or "conform" to this belief system in some shape or form.

Human beings prioritize acceptance. Most (if not all) people want acceptance by all. When people feel excluded, they feel unwanted, thus, have a need to feel wanted and included. And this is why this book has first explore some of the most relevant psychological studies on the construction of the Ego and on identity.

Darker-skinned races on the planet have suffered deeply for centuries, from this process of not being accepted. Even their "own" people of dark skin tones are "un-accepting" of dark skin tones. Ego needs to be in a safe place, and this may take the form of self-rejection and simultaneous gravitation towards what is accepted.

This process does not only apply to race. People, in general, want to be widely and openly accepted; if not, they inflict the hatred unto themselves then reject the people who remind them of those unacceptable, unlovable aspects of themselves. You cannot hate or resist anything without desiring something else. So, if dark people are rejecting their skin color, it means that there is a desire for whiteness or "non-blackness." This is an involuntary and unconscious subscription to a certain aspect of white supremacy.

Now there would not be a desire for whiteness without an existing belief that white is better. This would suggest that people have bought into "whiteness" as the standard and being better than "non-whiteness." Both whites and non-whites live by this ideal. All People are influenced by white supremacy in this way even the people who claim that they are not, which means that it is debatable that all people from all races are White Supremacists to an extent.

Of course, most people would dismiss this idea out of shame, guilt, and/or just not being self-aware enough to observe the workings of their subconscious minds and the opposing truth within it. This further supports my point that if racism (by the "Pro-black Interest Group's definition) is, in fact, "white supremacy", then everyone, including dark-skinned people, is racists.

Some may argue that hatred for one's race or color is not racism but simply, "self-hatred". While they are correct that there is some self-hatred involved, they are missing the point that it's both racism and self-hatred. One is driving the other. Racism projected outwards or within one's race is derived from some of the same kinds of emotional processes. They are both dealing with the same issue, both about race and the many intricacies within them. It's all "Race"-"ism".

If you call it color-ism or shade-ism, I can still refer to it as racism, because color and shade is a strong part of the concept of race. Not only can all kinds of racial negativity be considered racism, but they affect all races. Most people

[59]

probably would not agree or even fathom how it could be true that even white people suffer in this system of racism.

The people on the receiving end of oppression, discrimination, and abuse are in pain for sure; however, it takes considerable amounts of pain and hurt to inflict oppression, discrimination, and abuse unto others. The longer it takes to awaken to the fact that all people suffer emotionally with racism, the longer the pain of racism with lingering and even heighten. This is because, in addition to being ignorant of the suffering of those on the giving end, we continue to blame and shame them for the evils of the past and present.

Chapter 5 What is Anti-Racism?

Simplistically, anti-racism is being against racism. Many people can claim that they are against racism, but to be anti-racist requires much more than this. Many assimilationists are also against racism, but their unconscious biases remain unexamined as they attempt to address racism. They continue to operate from a place that centers white cultural norms and tries to incorporate minorities into society while maintaining white privilege.

Anti-racism requires a much more complex examination of our society, systems, and constructs. It actively works to identify racism in every portion of our society, learn how it operates to support our systems, and intentionally dismantle it so that we can build an equitable society. It demands more than tolerance; it demands inclusion and the removal of privilege, not as punishment but as fair. Anti-racism is the moral result of loving all those around them and wanting them to have access to every part of society at a level equal to the white majority.

Becoming anti-racist is a growth process that is not for the weak or the fearful. You may find yourself distanced political, socially, and morally from friends and family members that you were previously close to, as long as you remained silent. Despite this, you must remember that for minority groups, silence is not an option. Our very lives depend on people not remaining silent anymore.

Anti-racism is much more than being non-racist. Someone who is non-racist pats themselves on the back for not using a pejorative, but doesn't challenge others when they do. Non-racists champion specific causes that support people of color but never examine how their daily interactions may be filled with microaggressions toward those same people. Non-racism is very passive, while anti-racism is active and intentional. Non-racism supports systemic and individual racism throughout non-action, while anti-racism proactively seeks to dismantle each.

Non-racism means that you see that there is injustice present in our society, in our schools, in our institutions, and our neighborhoods, but you choose to do nothing about it. Your feeling that it is wrong does little to help because the oppressor is allowed to continue without any opposition from those who may have the power, voice, and resources to effectuate change.

To be anti-racist, you must be introspective and come to some realizations and understandings, but more than that, you must take action based upon your realizations. Below is the list of just a few ideas and action steps that I would like for you all to consider as you dive deeper into what it means to be an ally/accomplice in this fight against injustice.

Understand the foundations upon which racism is built. Many times, these racist policies were created to indulge someone's greed, and the racist ideas trickled down to common men who had no part in creating these policies. In understanding what racism is, we are also able to understand that the blatant acts of racism we see, such as the events of Charlottesville, and white people calling the police on black people for doing mundane actions, are just symptoms to a much larger system of racism. The far-right wingers like those in Charlottesville are dismissed as evil and racist, but I am certain that some of the people who called the cops on innocent black people would not have labeled themselves racists or placed themselves in the same category. However, regardless of severity and intent, each took racist actions as the result of the same ideas generated through racist policy.

Understanding what it means to be a person of color in this society means understanding what it means to be white. Whiteness is relational to blackness or Native American-ness or any other racial minority status. To attempt to understand one without examining the other is like attempting marriage counseling, but only discussing one spouse's concerns and issues. Whiteness is how structural advantages show up in our everyday life and experiences. By not examining whiteness, people ignore the ways that blackness and other minority experiences are caused by systemic racism and majority privilege. The tendency to not examine whiteness also allows for the continued insulation of white people from racial stress. Failure to examine whiteness in a segregated society leads to consistent and damaging misunderstandings of what it means to be a minority. The anti-racist is one who knows that reflectively examining their own experience is just as important as listening to others.

Being anti-racist does not mean being anti-white. We live in an either/or society. If you support something, it must mean that you are automatically against something. If the issue is related to race, people tend to attempt to appeal to white fears by making the "against" something that white people often greatly support.

One significant example of this is the Black Lives Matter movement. Though it was created after the death of Trayvon Martin, it came to the forefront after the death of Michael Brown in 2014. Black Lives Matter's sole purpose is to fight for an equitable society for people who look, which must include a justice system that values the lives of black people (even black criminals) as much as they do white people and criminals. They advocate for police accountability so that we can create a more equitable system. We can support both police and Black Lives Matter because they are not antithetical and should both be working together to create a safer society for all of us. Being pro-Black Lives Matter is not being anti-police. We must reject the idea that being anti-racist is being anti-white. Because of the connotations of the term "racism," some find it easy to assert that people speaking against it are simultaneously speaking against white people. We are instead speaking to toxic whiteness and the people who allow its damaging effects to go unchecked.

Push back against white supremacy and the people who knowingly or unknowingly perpetuate it. Once we develop a more thorough understanding of racism and have rid ourselves of the idea that extremists are only perpetuated, you must call it out when you see it. You should be the person who brings them relief because they know that you have made every effort to understand and to share in the task of getting other folks together on the issue of our humanity.

Confront racist notions where they live. You do not become anti-racist while performing community service in predominantly black neighborhoods. Your work as an anti-racist must be done in the institutions, neighborhoods, organizations, and systems where racist notions are incubated. Speaking to members of minority groups allows you to understand their experiences better and aids you in breaking down your own conscious and unconscious biases, which is necessary as you develop your anti-racism toolbox. However, you must take what you have learned back to your coworker, who constantly spouts discriminatory views of people of color or your church that is not very inclusive and continues to lose minority congregants. You must speak up in the PTA meetings and city council meetings. Otherwise, the work you do in the "hood" is merely placing a Band-Aid over a bullet wound.

Continuously learn. For every step you take, you should be learning all you can so that you can move to the next step and the one after that. If ever you get to a point where you think you've read it all, learned it all, or understand it all, you should probably turn back and start again at step one. We just cannot possibly learn everything, but we can do our best to be open to education on any subject. There is an infinite amount of knowledge out there for me to discover.

Be intentional in discussing race and discrimination with our children, family, and friends. Use your knowledge and courage to create more allies. The race is something that must confront and discuss every day.

Stand up for black children. Black and brown children are punished at a rate disproportionate to their white counterparts, beginning as early as kindergarten. Young black girls are viewed as less innocent than white children beginning as early as five years of age (Shapiro, "Study: Black Girls). Black children are less likely to receive trauma-informed care despite bearing the weight of both personal traumas as well as racial trauma. You have the power to provide support according to whatever resources you have. Anti-racism requires that we stand up for children of color in our schools, systems, and societies so that we plant seeds of acceptance, not rejection.

Do not hide behind whiteness when it is convenient. Remember that your black counterparts do not have the luxury of retreating when faced with racial hatred, microaggressions, or racial stress.

Let go of resources that are being hoarded in your neighborhoods, schools, and institutions.

Vote for political candidates who support policies that benefit all demographic groups. Call those politicians and hold them accountable for implementing change. We currently exist in a political atmosphere where there are politicians who are openly hostile to racial and religious minorities. Make your vote a conscious act of solidarity with the most vulnerable in our country. Understand the full impact of the policies you are voting for and research the individuals who are asking to represent you. Make sure they do not just represent some of us, but ALL of us, instead.

Support the economic development of minority businesses and communities. Our support helps them achieve that goal, as well as helps build generational wealth for African American families, something that our country's

[69]

policies have often prevented people in minority neighborhoods from doing.

Practice self-care and support your friends of color in their need for self-care, as well. You must regularly tend to your inner self. Spend time doing something you enjoy with friends who do not require emotional labor from me. Self-care looks different for everyone, but it should achieve the goal of helping you refocus on your purpose and recharge your socio-emotional battery.

As you dive deeper into the work of anti-racism, you will find that it is easier to differentiate between being non-racist and anti-racist. Your ultimate purpose should always be effectuating as much change as possible so that people of color have equal access to our society.

Chapter 6 What is Social Justice?

Social justice as a concept and practice was made necessary by the widespread injustice experienced by the majority of people on the planet. These injustices take many forms but seem to find a common link in the system of racism/White supremacy. In all areas of people activity, including economics, education, entertainment, labor, law, politics, religion, sex, and war/counter-war, each of the dividing lines are drawn with a colored pencil. For example, when exploring economic injustice and identify the gender gap regarding wages, It may see that even within the respective gender categories, there is an even more significant disparity that exists along the color-line. When a person looks at the wars that have happened on this planet, individuals will find that the most horrific and devastating versions are those waged against non-White peoples/nations by White peoples/nations. It is true whether we are speaking of the "war on drugs," or the Vietnam, Korean, or the various and on-going wars for control of resource-rich African nations. Education-based disparities are also distinguishable by race, more so than social, economic status, and parent education levels.

These disparities do not speak to the potential nor the innate attributes of non-White peoples. Instead, identify how the system skewed in such a way that it supports the progress of whites while actively stifling the progress of non-Whites. The mechanisms for impeding the progress of non-Whites can be challenging to identify because they are constantly changing form and becoming more sophisticated as the system continues to mature and refine itself. Refinement is the mechanism by which the tools of racism/White supremacy adjusted to render them more efficient, effective, less apparent, and even more acceptable by those who are negatively affected by their use. Amos Wilson often stated that the most effective systems of oppression, are those that associate oppression with a sense of progress and freedom, placing an invisible yoke on its victims.

Psychology specifically, and the social sciences generally, in regards to their ability to define mental health and its role in the determination of how to address, treat, and correct the same, gives it almost an unchecked ability to determine how people can and will live their lives. A person who does not understand this aspect of psychology will likely misunderstand much about life in general.

To properly begin the discussion, we must define the terms social and justice. Social means "relating to society or its organization." The word justice has many definitions, including, but not limited to, the following:

Fairness; Being just; moral rightness either inaction or attitude; righteousness; The fulfillment of what is, especially that which is merited, right, fair, moral or under the law; The upholding of what is, mainly fair treatment and due reward by standards, honor, or the law;

To gain a deeper understanding of the above definitions of justice, take a moment and look up the words used to define the concept, especially: moral, rightness, righteousness, just, fair, merited, law, reward, honor, standards, conformity, truth, fact, and, reason. The above definitions are highly subjective, meaning they can be altered and bent to fit particular political orientations, even those that may be damaging to others, and even unjust. This hypocrisy is what led Mr. Neely Fuller, Jr. to develop his definition of justice, which, in true counter-racist and compensatory fashion, is designed to produce a universally and mutually beneficial perspective of justice. His definition is:

"Making sure that those who need the most help get helped the most; and, guaranteeing that no one mistreated."

Notice how he makes no mention of law, nor of morality, legal, reasoning, and others. It has intentionally done as much as possible, remove those aspects of "justice" that can't be manipulated to produce injustice.

Social justice movements address their respective causes based on the above definitions, both in favor of how justice is represented in society, as well as in a challenge to how justice is itself, dealt with unjustly. This is an essential notion because many feel that "justice" has not been served when a police officer is found "not guilty" after murdering an unarmed victim. People feel that justice has not served because the killing was wrong, but courts rule that within the context of "the law," no crime has been committed. Therefore, they are not convicted. Again, according to the usual definitions, "justice" is the correct application of the law, which is a separate issue from determining the correctness of these laws.

The following five points, described by Sue & Sue in their Multicultural Counseling textbook, illustrate how the social justice perspective used to gain a new view on existing issues, by shifting the focus from the victims to the system, and the context within which they both exist:

- The locus of the predicament may reside in the social system (other learners, hostile campus situation, alienating curriculum, lack of opposition teachers/staff/students, and others) rather than in the individual.
- Behaviors that violate social norms may not be disordered or unhealthy.
- The group norms shared ideas, and institutional policies and practices that maintain the status quo may need to be challenged and changed.

- Prevention is a more efficient long-term solution.
- Organizational change requires a macrosystem approach involving other roles and skills beyond the traditional clinical one.

Using these five points provides a better way to frame the issues. People often identified as the issue and a pass given to the system they produced. A profound example is a pond where fish can be found to have deformities. An astute person should realize that the environment may be contaminated after pulling a few deformed fish from the water, thereby causing the observed malformations. This is the same for society. If a particular type of person or condition is continuously being produced, then there must be something in society producing it, intentionally, haphazardly, or in total ignorance.

Historically speaking, the need for social justice, as it relates to psychology, has been tirelessly fought for by some, and enthusiastically avoided by others. As previously mentioned, social justice movements and organizations are made necessary by the existence of injustice in the form of systemic racism/White supremacy. Therefore, the history of the United States of America is filled with examples of the intentional proliferation of injustice, and the rise of social justice movements designed to combat it. Examples are found in all areas of activity, including economics, education, entertainment, labor, law, politics, religion, sex, and war. Racism/White supremacy has effectively influenced each area with one precise and surgical cut from its most effective tool: the peculiar institution of chattel slavery.

Social justice movements are designed to address these issues, thereby providing several points of alignment between them. W. E. B. DuBois predicted "the problem of the color line" as the significant issue of the 20th century. He was correct as we can see that almost every point was drawn with a colored pencil, making racism the central injustice to be addressed. Psychiatry and other mental health-related jobs are the driving force propelling systematic injustice because they are the professions used to justify and create the injustices manifested in all other areas. The social justice perspective and approach becomes a necessity because of this. It is required to correctly define and work towards the manifestation of mental health amongst the oppressed.

Establishing social justice requires that we identify areas wherein equal access and opportunities have been limited and adversely impacted by laws inhibiting certain groups from learning of, and utilizing rights and resources that are guaranteed with relative ease to others. Redlining in the housing market stands as a prominent example of such practices. Segregated hospitals and schools also exemplify this practice, especially when these public institutions never became "separate but equal."

Social justice programs with an agenda for acquiring justice in mental health will also consider, and base their platforms on, the need for a socially-just perspective of psychological assessment, diagnosis, and treatment. If individual practitioners are wedded to the deficit model and the structural racism upon which the field of psychology and psychiatry are built, then they are more likely to perpetuate injustices through their daily practice. This translates into the disproportionate misdiagnosis and subsequent mistreatment of non-White populations. This makes for an almost inescapable loop of economic-, education-, and legal-based hardships. To misdiagnose is to set one up for mistreatment, to mistreat is to leave the actual issues unaddressed, while creating new harm;

this is often labeled "benign neglect" or treated as the result of implicit bias, but maybe intentionally employed for more sinister purposes.

Chapter 7 Kids Reaction to Diversity

Are little kids inquisitive of characteristics about racial, physical, and cultural? Is it safe to say that they are aware of racism? Children are a lot aware of racial differences. Many are additionally aware of racism. Notwithstanding, to read by far most of the writings on kid improvement and youth training, one could never predict it. No notice at all is made in these writings of how little kids build up their very own understanding and others' racial and cultural characters.

The silence of these texts, which are used to prepare Teachers, Clinicians, Social Specialists, and different experts, reflect and sustain an overall majority culture belief system - that children are "color-blind," for example, they aren't aware of the race as well as the racism. This philosophy further accepts that if grown-ups don't chat with children about "it," children will be non-prejudiced grown-ups once they grow up. For swearing and evasion, at that point, seem, by all accounts, to be the principal methods for managing one of the most inescapable and vital issues of U.S. society.

The "color-blind" position is comparable to the ostrich's head-in-the-sand methodology. An impressive collection of research shows that children in the U.S. know, at an early age, of physical and cultural differences among individuals, and they learn the overarching social perspectives toward these distinctions whether they are in direct contact with individuals not quite the same as themselves.

In the given example, Mary Ellen Goodman, in the wake of mentioning broad objective facts of 100 Black and white children, with ages 3 to 5, only 26 percent of the children in her example were communicating strongly entrenched race-related qualities by the age of four after announcing that racial awareness was available. A great part of the research has likewise investigated the impacts that individual and institutional racism in U.S. society has on children's self-ideas.

These examinations show that Third World children's confidence can be genuinely hurt, however, a few investigators make a qualification between a child's sure confidence cultivated by family and community and a kid's developing awareness of the racist mentalities and practices of the majority society. White children are additionally dehumanized and harmed mentally by racism.

The prejudices of their general public were still particularly with them, however, they had it penetrated them that it was 'not ideal' to communicate such emotions." Moreover, as Abraham F. Citron appropriately sums up the issue: White centeredness isn't the truth of [the white child's world, yet he is under the hallucination that it is. It is along these lines incomprehensible for him to bargain precisely or enough with the universe of human and social connections... Children who create along these lines are ransacked of chances for passionate and scholarly development, hindered in the fundamental improvement of oneself, with the goal that they can't be understanding or acknowledge mankind. This is a character result in which it is very conceivable to incorporate with children an incredible inclination and empathy for creatures and an oblivious dread and dismissal of contrasting individuals. Such people are in no way, shape, or form arranged to live and move with either gratefulness or adequacy in this day and age.

Building a positive and learned racial/cultural identity is one of a Third World kid's major formative assignments in our racist society. This undertaking is similarly significant however to some degree diverse for white children. Many white families don't well-spoken that they have a racial identity. As Judy Katz composes: The unrivaled demeanor, "white is right," regularly leaves whites befuddled about their identity. ...Since the United States, culture is fixated on white standards, white individuals once in a while need to deal with that part of their identity.

White individuals don't consider themselves to be white. This is a method of rejecting the obligation for propagating the racist framework and being part of the issue. By observing oneself exclusively as an individual, one can abandon one's racism. The absence of understanding of self-attributable to a poor feeling of identity makes whites build up a negative mentality toward minorities on both a cognizant and an oblivious level. Fundamental to the development of one's identity in U.S. society is learning how to manage racism.

For children of groups mistreated by racism, the undertaking is learning to battle against its effect. For white children, it is practicing to be anti-racist. The "color-blind" proposal isn't just false; it has a few vindictive angles. In any event, this idea is counter-gainful, in light of the fact that while parents, teachers, and others are quiet about racism, and children are attempting to understand their encounters. Besides, "color-blind" is a point of view that infers that distinctions are terrible because it centers only on the all-inclusiveness of people.

Further, the belief system of "color-visual deficiency" grants individuals to prevent the job from securing institutional racism. By affirming that racism is brought about by recognizing differences, as opposed to by a social framework that misuses certain racial groups for economic benefit, "color-blind" really bolsters the racist business as usual.

As Ann Beuf brings up, the "color-blind" postulation infers that lone family socialization impacts a kid's feeling of self, and it in this manner "permits whites and white organizations to get away from the outcomes of existing basic game plans." She proceeds: On the other hand, parental preparing which repudiates ["color-blind" ideologies] can assume an essential job in building up positive racial perspectives in children... Our information with the children of activists proposes that a home where the positive estimation of [one's group] is focused will deliver children who feel positive about their gathering. Children will "normally" grow up to be non-racist grown-ups just when they live in a non-racist society. Up to that point, grown-ups must guide children's antiracist advancement. This will incorporate the cultivating of:

- Precise information and pride about one's racial/cultural identity.
- Precise information and valuation for other racial groups; and
- An understanding of how racism works and how to battle it.

[86]

The initial phase in this procedure is to acknowledge the way that a procedure is required. The subsequent advance is to see how children consider racial issues at various stages in their turn of events. Toward this end, we went through two years gathering information from parents and Teachers about the sort of inquiries and remarks children present at various age levels. We have used the system recommended by Piaget's psychological improvement hypothesis in our investigation, as we trust it helps with seeming well and good out of children's observations and encounters and empowers us to encourage their learning.

Chapter 8 Help Children about Their Curiosity And Question

There are times when we as guardians must clarify things that are difficult and uncalled for bigotry, sexism, generalizations, detest. Times, when we should comfort our kids, times you have needed to help your 10-year-old child, discover that what some would do unto him isn't continuously kind or reasonable.

Talk transparently

At the point when we are straightforward with youngsters about our nation's history of bias, sexism, and generalizations, we help set them up to challenge these issues when they emerge.

A youngster who knows the racial history of the Confederate banner, for instance, is less prone to wield that image out of obliviousness.

Model value

As guardians, we are our children's first instructors. With regards to instructing resistance, activities express stronger than words. At the point when you state that young men and young ladies are equivalent yet decline to purchase your child an Easy Bake Oven since it's a "young ladies' toy," what message do you send?

Accomplish something

Stand firm when you witness the foul play. Challenge prejudice, fanaticism what's more, generalizations, and urge your youngster to make a move, as well. Quietness and inaction in the essence of bias overlook. Concerning hostile mascots, for instance, hold a request drive, compose an article in the school paper, sort out a blacklist of the school gracefully store, plan something for having any kind of effect.

These discussions are seldom simple, and some of the time we don't have answers. What we do have is time, tolerance, and the craving to enable our youngsters to develop into grown-ups who esteem, what's more, respect decent variety. So, sometime in the future, they may recollect what we said the night before they began first grade — and be better individuals for it.

Mutual understanding through interaction

Expanding communication skills to develop understanding, clarity, and focus created mutual understanding among people.

Communication and listening

These fundamental skills that look so simple on the surface but it seem so difficult to understand at the moments of reckoning. It's a two-way process wherein one of the constant challenges in home settings and work. Learn to build understanding while overcoming the hurdles to "communicating".

Creating mutual understanding requires:

- Listening to others.

- Understanding the significance of a person's styles and hurdles to efficient communication.

- Practicing skills in questioning as well as listening.

- Building collective transparency and understanding.

- Enhancing the ability to cope with irritation and frustration.

When two strangers come across and communicate in their first encounter, the degree of the development of their mutual understanding can determine by how deep their conversations, psychologists have discovered.

Personal identity as well as mutual understanding said to be the main outcome of interpersonal interaction and communication. Interpersonal relationships' explanatory accounts have to be increased by considering ethical problems that are raised.

The ability to effectively communicate with all people in an organization is a fundamental skill that all leaders must learn to master. Effective communication is knowing about what, when, and to whom information is shared. It is also an assessment of sensitivity to the manner in which the receiver will optimally understand the message.

Rather than explaining communication, let us define that effective communication is said to be an interaction ceasing in mutual understanding. This definition, when using it the right way when communicating and interacting requires some flexibility. It will make every interaction a collective effort. To make sure understanding, there is no one way. It will require an investment to have genuine communication in each other sides of the conversation such as using nonverbal cues, speaking, and actively listening. If all are working on the subject of mutual understanding, they will be adaptable to how they will communicate, and they will listen for the clarification of meaning and such.

Groups come down with a thorough discussion of ways of solving a given issue, highlighting the group's objectives, and coming at a plan and a goal on how to attain the milestone intellectually. This is said to be true at a lot of stages, from neighborhood organizations to corporate administrative teams up to the cabinet meeting of the President. Nevertheless, this kind of decision-making structure faces more challenges than acknowledging it in general. These processes are often indeterminate, haphazard, and incomplete.

The heightening interdependence between today's' nations makes it's the most important rationale in promoting broader mutual understanding among people internationally. Hence, to have a truly peaceful environment, the need to intensify the mutual understanding between heritages of different is also important.

The world's leading nations are yielding efforts to extend their role in recognizing the value of cultural interchange together with the government-related associations and other non-government organizations doing a wide variety of activities. The creativity as well as the inventiveness of the private sector must be utilized the fullest, especially in undertaking a wide variety of activities in cultural interchange and several other factors that are needed for implementing of cultural activities limit. Being entirely aware of the significance of cultural interchange, the Government is striving in promoting a valuable and well-balanced program of cultural interchange and providing assistance to the cultural interchange programs of the private organizations.

Chapter 9 How to Raise Anti-Racism and Social Justice Children

As social media and individuals around the word detonate with indignation regarding the murdering of one more black man on account of the police, stressed guardians battle with how to safeguard their kids from seeing the most terrible of the brutality while all the while clarifying the desolates of racism. It couldn't have come at a more terrible time.

Shielding at home for a considerable length of time to maintain a strategic distance from the dangers of the pandemic COVID-19, numerous guardians worried by shuffling work and kid care from home had facilitated their limitations on screen time for their kids.

Presently almost certainly, children may discover the video of George Floyd, an unarmed and bound dark man in Minneapolis, panting for breath as a white cop squeezed a knee into his neck.

Expert states that guardians ought to assume their youngsters are now mindful of catastrophes like these and their repercussions. Regardless of whether from online life accounts, discussions with companions or guardians, caught discussions, or the misery they observe in the essences of those they love, youngsters recognize what is happening without the direction and approval of their parental figures, they might be exploring their sentiments alone.

Take Care of You First

By what method can a parent help their kid cross these upsetting occasions?

Allow the youngster's age and level of improvement to be your guide, on the whole, be certain that you are in the correct outlook. A parent's initial step is to deal with themselves, their psychological wellness, and their enthusiastic wellbeing. Put on their oxygen mask on first before they put the oxygen mask on their youngster. This doesn't mean relinquishing the outrage or nervousness, it just methods arranging it better so you can think and act all the more plainly.

When a parent is completely accessible to be a quiet, reasonable voice, at that point you can parse out what's imperative to pass onto your youngster with the goal that you're not oversharing information that may additionally damage them or cause them to feel uncertain or perilous.

Infants and Toddlers

While youngsters younger than three won't comprehend what's going on TV, they will have the option to get on the dread, direness, or outrage in individuals' voices and practices.

At this age, stress appears in fastidious or unregulated conduct. To shield that from happening, guardians should peruse, tune in to or watch the news when the infant isn't truly there.

Watch what you have to remain educated about your locale, however then turn it off and accomplish something that causes your family to feel whole and connected. You may need to reground yourself or manage your considerations and emotions before reconnecting with your children. This is an ideal opportunity to start showing your youngster fundamental prejudice and how to distinguish and invalidate it.

Racist generalizations and inclination start at an incredibly youthful age. As right on time as a half year, an infant's cerebrum can see race-based contrasts and can disguise racial predisposition by age two to four.

"Learning" racism is a great deal like learning another dialect for children and little children. It can occur without parental information, just by the racial generalizations so predominant in the public eye.

By age 12, numerous kids become set in their convictions. That allows guardians "10 years to form the learning procedure, with the goal that it diminishes racial predisposition and improves social comprehension," they composed. While accommodating for all races, it's particularly significant for white kids to see earthy colored and dark children in a positive light to battle foundational bigotry, expert state. Books that profile multi-racial characters are a magnificent route for guardians to do that. What's more, since it's never too soon to read to an infant, start immediately.

Presence of mind Media, a non-benefit that rates movies, TV shows, books, applications, and other media for guardians and schools, has curated a rundown of 80 books with different, multi-social characters for preschoolers and more seasoned, some of which could without much of a stretch be appropriate for children and little children. There's likewise a site called the Brown Bookshelf, These are books that have, earthy colored and dark heroes who manage intense issues. I think books are incredibly principal, particularly for more youthful children.

Preschool and Elementary Ages

This is the age when children start to ask questions on for what valid reason others appear to be unique than they do. If your kid gets some information about somebody's skin tone, you may state, 'Isn't it brilliant that we are on the whole so extraordinary!' You can even hold your arm against theirs to show the distinctions in skin tones in your family. At this age, youngsters will see and assimilate upsetting pictures from fights and mobs actually, likely concentrating on agonizing over a consuming van or an unnerving glancing individual in a mask. Guardians ought to give a valiant effort to confine the exposure kids this age have to media, regardless of whether TV, PDAs or tablets, specialists state.

This should be possible by setting certain occasions that youngsters can utilize their gadgets, co-see the substance with their kids, find different exercises like playing outside, games, cooking together, set principles that children should utilize the gadgets in a typical zone where guardians can check-in. These occasions likewise give chances to guardians to show the conduct they need their children to follow by additionally constraining their exposure to media.

Be that as it may, kids will probably have just caught grown-up discussions, or been presented to what's going on through social media records and discussions with companions. Guardians who have not as of now, ought to proactively draw in their children around these upsetting occasions. You should ask them what they know and what they've seen. Ask them how they are feeling. Approve their emotions and let them realize what you are doing to protect them - be it in your home or your locale.

Guardians will likewise need to give their youngsters the more extensive cultural setting of prejudice to attempt to clarify the fury of protestors filling the roads of urban areas the country over. Thusly, guardians can help in building sympathy and show the point of view taking, as opposed to concentrating on the kid's particular feelings of trepidation.

Rather than concentrating on questions the youngster may have about concrete things, ask them questions like 'How would you think those individuals were feeling? Do you know why they were furious? What do you do when you feel like something is unjustifiable?

Giving a controlled space to comprehend what is happening and approaches to process it will assist kids with exploring the upsetting feelings, weakness, and dread they might be encountering. Age-proper books that manage segregation and clarify sentiments from alternate points of view are amazingly useful during this time, expert state.

You can likewise give them videos of serene protests from the past, where individuals were motivated to request fair treatment while cautioning that some YouTube videos can contain extreme political and disinformation advertisements happening before and during videos.

Simply avoid those advertisements and begin showing your little youngsters the Martin Luther King Jr. or other videos once the advertisement has passed. For older kids, you can ask them what they think from various advertisements and whether they're dependable.

Tweens and Teens

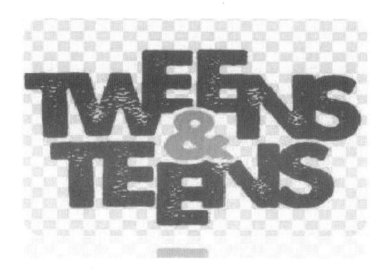

Tweens and teenagers will probably be seeing all the inclusion of police mercilessness and protests on their cell phones. Most adolescents get comfort by speaking with their companions via social media. A few teenagers have even started taking an interest in online activism.

Online activism is an adapting response for certain young people, particularly at present while we're physically far off. Reposting, re-tweeting, communicating how they're feeling, talking with companions has been useful, kind of a functioning sort of adapting reaction.

Different teenagers, particularly those that are not of a minority foundation, so those that are white, are instructing themselves concerning why this is occurring, what's the historical backdrop of our nation, what's going on the present moment. Intellectualizing the issues has been useful for them to comprehend that this isn't only a present-day issue, this has been continuing for a considerable length of time.

At this age, children will have the option to contemplate racism, treachery, and fierce versus protest done peacefully and then speak their views with their guardians, experts state.

Guardians can ask their tweens or adolescents whether they've seen anything on the internet about the uproars and fights, what they think, and shouldn't something be said about it been upsetting or inspiring.

As the parent of an adolescent will verify, the direct questioning of youngsters regularly doesn't deliver useful reactions. A typical response parent might get is "I don't know," so expert recommends guardians additionally have a go at getting some information about the kinds of unfairness kids to see or feel in their regular day to day existences.

Guardians can likewise utilize documentaries and good movies that can teach older teenagers on the historical backdrop of segregation. You don't have to lecture youngsters about what is 'correct' or 'wrong, expert states. It's smarter to have a discussion where they go to their understanding and can see things in a bigger social setting.

Kira Banks, a clinical therapist whose website "Raising Equity" gives free movies and assets on how guardians can battle racism and develop a receptive outlook in themselves and their children, proposes guardians watch movies like "13th," an amazing glance at institutional prejudice in the equity framework that debuted in 2016 to overwhelming applause at the New York Film Festival.

People need to teach their children about the historical backdrop of racism, the work must be done by every single social class and race, expert state, including the most advantaged.

White and non-dark families ought not to shield their older kids from these pictures. We have to connect with our youngsters in a discussion about bigotry and utilize these occasions as an impetus.

While it is upsetting to watch, we have to sit with that distress and show our families how to channel that vitality to function to disassemble the racist structures that exist in our vicinity.

Chapter 10 Parents Right Examples to Anti-Racism

To make an equivalent society, we should focus on settling on unbiased decisions and being antiracist in all parts of our lives. In a racist society, it isn't sufficient to be non-racist, we should be anti-racist.

Race doesn't biologically exist, yet how we relate to race is so incredible, it impacts our encounters and shapes our lives. In a general public that benefits white individuals and whiteness, racist thoughts are viewed as ordinary all through our media, culture, social frameworks, and organizations. Truly, racist sees supported the uncalled for treatment and persecution of minorities (counting subjugation, isolation, internment, and so forth.). We can be persuaded that racism is just about individual attitudes and activities, yet racist approaches likewise add to our polarization. While individual decisions are harming, racist thoughts in strategy have a wide-spread effect by undermining the value of our frameworks and the reasonableness of our institution. To make an equivalent society, we should focus on settling on fair-minded decisions and being antiracist in all parts of our lives.

Being antiracist is battling against racism. Racism takes a few structures and works regularly couple with at any rate one other structure to fortify racist thoughts, conduct, and approach.

Nobody is brought into the world racist or antiracist; these outcomes from the decisions we make. Being antiracist results from a cognizant choice to make a visit, steady, impartial decisions day by day. These decisions require continuous mindfulness and self-reflection as we travel through life. Without settling on antiracist decisions, we (un)consciously maintain parts of racial oppression, white-prevailing society, and inconsistent organizations and society. Being racist or antiracist isn't about what your identity is; it is about what you do.

What do the components of learning recorded above intend to you?

Creating schedules to settle on antiracist decisions is a day by day duty that must be done with expectations. The proceeded with endeavors of every one of us exclusively can indicate an enduring change in our general public. Since racism works at different levels, we need to settle on antiracist decisions at the different levels - individual, relational, and institutional - to annihilate racism from the structures and texture of our general public. In "How to Be an Antiracist," Dr. Ibram Kendo expresses, "[We must] put stock in the likelihood that we can endeavor to be antiracist from this day forward. Put stock in the likelihood that we can change our social orders to be antiracist from this day forward. Racist power isn't faithful. Racist arrangements are not indestructible. Racial disparities are not unavoidable. Racist thoughts are not normal to the human psyche."

[113]

Different Ways to Be Antiracist

- **Understand the meaning of racist.**

Discussions about racism regularly endure when members can't characterize the importance of the word. Merriam-Webster characterizes racism as "a conviction that race is the essential determinant of human attributes and limits and that racial difference produces an inalienable prevalence of a specific race." Few individuals would concede that definition mirrors their perspectives yet all things considered deliberately or accidentally have faith in or underwrite racist thoughts.

Kendi goes further, characterizing the word racist as: "One who is supporting a racist strategy through their activities or inaction or communicating a racist thought." This sharp definition powers the peruser to consider themselves responsible for their thoughts and activities.

An antiracist composes Kendi is "One who is supporting an antiracist approach through their activities or communicating an antiracist thought."

- **Stop saying "I'm not racist."**

It's insufficient to state, "I'm not racist," and frequently it's a self-serving opinion. Kendi says individuals continually change the meaning of what's racist so it doesn't concern them. On the off chance that you're a white patriot who's not savage, says Kendi, at that point you may see the Ku Klux Klan as racist. In case you're a Democrat who believes there's something socially wrong with dark individuals, at that point racists to you may be individuals who are Republicans.

In this way, for instance, in case you're a white liberal who sees herself as "not racist" however you won't send your kid to a nearby government-funded school in light of the fact that the populace is dominatingly African American, that decision is racist. The antiracist position would be to at any rate consider enlisting your kid or potentially finding out about the incongruities and disparities influencing that school to battle them.

- **Identify racial imbalances and differences.**

Racism yields racial imbalances and aberrations in each segment of private and open life. That remembers for legislative issues, human services, criminal equity, instruction, salary, work, and home possession. Being antiracist implies finding out about and recognizing imbalances and aberrations that give, specifically, white individuals, or any racial gathering, material focal points over non-white individuals.

At the point when Social Security was made in 1935, for instance, it prohibited residential and horticultural laborers, most of whom were dark. While the Social Security Administration denies racial predisposition was a factor in that choice, it despite everything implied that dark laborers had less open door through the span of decades to collect investment funds and riches contrasted with white specialists. Different strategies that excessively gave "charge financed riches building openings" to white Americans created comparative outcomes for dark Americans.

So a racist examination would attribute poor or more regrettable results for dark Americans to the gathering's conduct or qualities. An antiracist examination would clarify that the issue isn't the gathering, however, the approaches that put racial gatherings at an unmistakable drawback.

- **Confront the racist thoughts you've held or kept on holding.**

When you've started distinguishing racial differences, look at whether your perspectives, convictions, or casting ballot designs have legitimized racial disparity.

In case you're the parent who won't send a youngster to a transcendently dark school, consider how that decision impacts your perspectives on discipline approaches and contract schools, the arrangement gives that are profoundly interwoven with race and racism. Do you vote in favor of educational committee or city board up-and-comers who would prefer not to address instructive aberrations or neutralize nearby supporters attempting to increment instructive value? Do you realize that subsidizing arrangements influence how assets are allotted to schools and why those practices can make racial variations? To numerous individuals, these real factors most likely appear to be separated from whether they're racist, however, Kendi contends that staying uninformed about them, or declining to change strategies that produce inconsistencies, isn't a possibility for somebody who needs to be antiracist.

Kendi's excursion shows that individuals can hold racist thoughts without acknowledging they're one-sided — and keeping in mind that they grasp thoughts that are antiracist. On the off chance that you don't know whether your convictions or perspectives are racist, tune in to forefront racial equity backers, activists, and associations that have laid out antiracist positions and arrangements. Let that listening brief further reflection concerning why you've had faith in specific thoughts.

- **Understand how your antiracism should be intersectional.**

Kendi contends that racist thoughts and strategies target a wide range of individuals inside racial gatherings. A strategy that makes disparity among white and Native American individuals, for instance, likewise yields an imbalance between white men and Native American ladies. If one accepts that dark men are better than dark ladies, at that point that individual won't have the option to perceive how certain thoughts and strategies excessively influence dark ladies in unsafe manners.

Since race converges with various parts of individuals' personalities, including their sex, sexuality, and ethnicity, it's basic to utilize an intersectional approach while being antiracist.

- **Champion antiracist thoughts and strategies**

One can't endeavor to be antiracist without activity, and Kendi says that a single direction to act is by supporting associations in your locale that are battling approaches that make racial differences. You can chip in for or finance those associations. Kendi likewise suggests utilizing one's capacity or getting into a place of capacity to change racist approaches in any setting where they exist — school, work, government, etc. The fact of the matter is to focus on some type of activity that can change racist approaches.

Chapter 11 Solidarity against Racism

Solidarity work can restructure resource distribution and power differentials. It implies that you have skills to offer, and constantly and consciously working towards developing others' leadership and access to resources. This process includes building valuable relationships, political advocacy, being transparent in actions, reallocating resources, and being sustainable and strategic. The term "accountability" means supporting people and their projects.

The biggest personal challenges were overcoming ego and Eurocentric cultural traditions. Sometimes, individuals made a momentous number of mistakes but in effect, learned a thousand precious lessons. The biggest mistake maybe was losing sight of the importance of building valuable relationships. From day one, prioritized work over friendship and ultimately limited the long-lasting impact and relationships that you might still have today if you've acted differently. It is one that prioritizes leadership development and ensures that this work continues to new generations.

Implementing a Racist-Free Environment

As racism is such a vile and inhumane practice, it is best to make sure that such behavior is removed from areas of society, such as in schools, work, businesses, and such. Implementing a racism-free environment through personal effort is the key to accomplishing this.

Eliminating Racism in Schools

The first location to introduce the elimination of racist ideas is in school. Molding children's minds into an open acceptance of the difference in culture and appearance in people are huge for the future of the world. One can start introducing racial acceptance by including in curriculums the achievements of various cultures.

Teachers can introduce small historical snippets of famous people from all over the world; cite their achievements and how they contributed to society. By showing students the achievement made by every culture on Earth, they can see that no one is inferior, as everyone is equally capable of achieving great deeds if given the chance.

One thing teachers or parents should stress is that people are usually a product of their environment more than any other factor out there. For example, if you were born into a single-parent, low-income household, then you are more likely to be involved in criminal activity during your youth, then a person who was born into a wealthy, strong-knit family.

This is not always the case, but the correlation is undeniable. It is the reason why we must strive to strengthen all families and friendships because the more connected people feel, the better they will perform in all aspects of their life.

It is not a less-fortunate child's fault if they are struggling to find discipline in their life with all the chips stacked against them. It is the job of the communities and schools to work on bridging this gap so that when the less-fortunate children grow up, they are educated enough to break the cycle of low-opportunity.

Bullying

Though bullying is not confined to racist behavior, there are many cases where people are bullied because of racial differences. Asians, Indians, and Middle Eastern students are often the target of racial bullying. This is especially so with people from Muslim countries because of the improper association made between Islamic traditions and terrorism.

It is very important to address incidents of bullying promptly, especially if the reasons are racial. It is vital to educate bullies to respect people as they are, and not by their race. It is also important to implement sanctions for such degrading activity.

Simple Methods to Prevent Racial Discrimination in Classrooms

Create activities that will allow students to communicate with each other. Students need to know each other on a deeper level than just viewing each other as classmates. Include movies that deal with racism among the "must watch" videos in class.

Introduce anti-racism heroes and inform students of their struggles against discrimination and how they became pillars in anti-racism movements.

Eliminating Racism in the Workplace

Racism can occur in large multi-national corporations or even in the small grocery stores and shops that are just around the corner. Discrimination and racist activity at the workplace may come from a workmate, supervisor, or even from customers.

However, to eliminate racism, one must transform the workplace into an area that is friendly to all cultures. These are some tips on how to transform the workplace into a place where racial discrimination is minimal or non-existent:

Managers should create anti-racism policies that employees should adhere to. This set of rules should be separate from the national law and be more unique in its approach. Each company should have its policies that the employees work to create. By incorporating the involvement of the employees, there will be more investment from them to abide by the rules.

Instill in employees that promotions are based on skill and performance and not by racial or gender preference. If possible, conduct team building activities that will create a stronger bond between employees (especially between those of different nationalities).

Eliminating Racism in Society

Destroying racism and racial discrimination from society may be a hard thing to accomplish, but it is not impossible. The need to break patterns of racism and the cultural barrier it produces is vital for societies to improve and advance.

One should always remember that humankind is just a single species and everyone is connected. Though people are different in many ways, these differences are only skin deep and inside each person on Earth, resides a unique individual that deserves love and respect.

People often get frustrated and feel that they have no control over racism in society. This is not true, however, because the only thing you can control is your influence in the world. You can always be a great example to others by being articulate, educated, and a productive member of society. By being an influential individual, you will begin to empower those around you to achieve great things and most importantly, you will slowly break down the barriers in society.

If you feel that someone is being racist towards you, the most productive way to handle it is to address the fact that you heard or saw the racist behavior. Stay calm and polite and don't let your emotions get in the way of relaying a message.

Remember, the reason the person or group is being racist towards you is that they are either ignorant of your culture or they feel threatened by your success. The way to handle this is not to make them feel more threatened or scared. You must cherish the opportunity to enlighten someone and handle it with class.

After addressing the behavior, make sure to tell the person that you felt uncomfortable by the act of racism and that you would love to answer any questions that he/she may have about your race. By creating this almost awkward situation, you are forcing dialogue between you and the discriminator. Do not let the opportunity pass to encourage the person to speak his/her mind. It may be the only chance of communication this person will ever have to express something like this.

At this point, the discriminator will usually apologize. However, some will not feel bad about their discrimination and will give you reasons for their beliefs. While they are giving you their explanation, try your best to avoid a knee-jerk reaction or even worse, insulting them back.

Fighting discrimination with discrimination never works when dealing with racism. The best solution is to see to it that a proper dialogue occurs between the two parties involved. By being able to explain why oppression happens and why people mustn't stick to discriminatory behavior, you might just be able to sway the other person to the side of peace and equality.

If possible, try to create some type of contact with this person for future reference. Explain to them that you would like to show them that judging someone negatively based on skin color or cultural background is silly. Do your best to prove that people have the same tendencies, no matter the race, it is just that we all have different opportunities which shape our behaviors.

A great way to help the person overcome their racist issues is to invite them to see your culture. This will shock most people who are racist. They will be forced to either learn more or to publicly accept that they are choosing to remain ignorant.

You may also realize that racism is born out of a culture that is intolerant of things that exist outside the person's common education, and by inviting people who enjoy the privilege to see the world outside their comfort zones, they will understand how problematic a discriminatory worldview is.

Now with all the guidelines for how to handle a situation involving racism, you may be thinking, why should I have to do so much just to get equal respect?

This goes back to the fact that many racist people are a product of their environment as well. Maybe they had nobody close to them to teach them about acceptance. Maybe they never knew a person of your race, or maybe they had one experience which turned out to be negative.

Whatever the case, you should remember that it is not necessarily about changing that one person's perception, although that is valuable in itself. It is more about the possible impact it will have on the world. If you can help that one person, how will that affect his/her interactions with other people of your race? How will it benefit his/her children, grandchildren, social circles, etc.?

Be the best example you can be, and the rest will fall into place. You cannot force another person to change, but you can hold up the mirror to their face with your kindness and influence.

Chapter 12 Racism and Race Tool

I t is inaccurate to treat people differently because of their race or culture. If it happens to you, remember no one has the proper to make you feel bad or abuse who you are. Racial harassment is a type of racism where someone's harassment makes a specialty of race, ethnicity, or culture. Racism and racial intimidation are wrong and you could get help to prevent it.

- Racism and racist bullying may also include:
- Being referred to as racist names or sending insults or threats.
- Having to harm your belongings or see racist graffiti

- .Personal attacks, together with violence or attack.

- Exclusion, different treatment, or exclusion.

- People who make assumptions about you because of your color, race, or culture.

- Making you feel like you need to change your look.

- Racist jokes, along with jokes approximately your race, race, or culture.

Racism can affect everyone. It can make you sense that you are no longer vital or do not suit in. You may also sense sad, depressed, or angry. Even when not directed at you, it can be affected as in case you heard a person discriminating towards their culture.

4 Things to Remember:

- It is unlawful to treat a person otherwise or unfairly due to his race.

- Racism and racial intimidation are wrong, although one doesn't realize they're doing it.

- If someone commits a crime in opposition to you because of your race, religion, or culture, its miles a hate crime.

- You aren't by me and there are ways to get support.

What Can You Do?

If someone calls you via name, scares you, or acts unfairly, you may get assist to forestall this:

- Go away: If a person is racist in the direction of you right now, stay away and don't retaliate or respond to live secure

- Tell a person what's going on: This may want to him your teacher, your sports activities attain , or your supervisor at work. Remember that you can always talk to a person's manager approximately racism 'anyplace you are.

- Stay secure: Walk from school or college with a person you know and maintain your telephone charged. Calls to the emergency numbers are free.

[133]

- Stay secure online: Change
  your privacy settings, document abuse at
  the website or app, and block customers who bully
  you or discriminate remarks or threats.

- Keep tune of it: Messages, videos, or a diary of
  what's taking place can help an adult or as evidence.

- Keep pronouncing it: You can also need to
  speak greater than once approximately racism or
  racist harassment. If you do now not think they
  are serious, it's far appropriate to
  inform someone else.

- Find someone to help you: It may also take time
  to stop bullying. If you
  think an instructor does not want to help
  you can talk to the supervisor.

- Every college should have anti-
  bullying coverage to shield you. If
  your college doesn't assist, you can tell the police.
  Tell the police: If you sense threatened or
  have committed a crime, you can file 999 to the
  police in an emergency or 101 to the police later.

How to Help A Friend:

If you spot or pay attention to racism, racist harassment, or discrimination, there are ways you can help:

- Offer your assist and inform your pal that what befell to them changed into wrong
- Ask your pal if he wants to document the incident. You also can provide to testify if you experience secure and comfortable.
- Call the emergency services if you want the police or ambulance to keep your pal secure.
- Take notice of what you notice and listen as quickly as possible. This may be used as evidence or, if necessary, to make a police statement.
- If it's safe to do so, talk. Keep calm and be assertive. You can say that you disagree with racist remarks or jokes.

Why Are People Racist:

Our minds and ideals grow as they develop and are influenced by utilizing what we see
and study in pals and family, neighborhoods, schools, and the media.
People who grow up in a family wherein racist views are expressed or who're racist jokes can discover ways to agree with that racism is ordinary and acceptable.
An opportunity to engage with
people, mainly from other cultures or origins. Racism can from time to time begin in response to world activities or news.
Other times, a certain racial man or woman who has had a painful personal enjoyment with a rupee can blame anybody in that race. Everyone makes assumptions. This can occur when they have no danger of triumphing over alternative opinions.
It is never appropriate to discriminate against a person by using race. If you are concerned about how
your views may affect different people, it may be useful to imagine that you are someone else to attempt to see
their views.

Speaking On Racism:

There are things you may do to talk approximately racism and racist harassment:

- Treat people pretty and with respect: We all make assumptions, so try to notice the whole thing you do and treat each person as individuals

- Don't be given racist jokes: Some men and women can make racist jokes look good. Racist jokes are a kind of abuse and those may be injured even though they don't display that they are upset at the moment.

- Learn approximately other cultures and nationalities.

- If your pals are afraid to talk approximately it, ask about their tradition or history for extra informatio.

- Raising consciousness of racism and racist harassment.

- Participate in meetings and campaigns and educate others on the outcomes of racism.

- Talk approximately your experiences whilst you are safe and supported, or on message boards.

- Talk about your feelings.

- If you experience, see or hear something offensive, communicate to someone you trust, along

[137]

with your friends, family, or teacher. Or you could talk to a Childline counselor.

Conclusion

The race is powerful nonsense!

— (Dismantling Racism Workshop, Race Matters for Juvenile Justice, Charlotte, NC)

Are the blank spaces that were reserved for note-taking and reflective journaling now overflowing with your notes, personal reflections, answers, and others? Do you have more questions?

The impact of racism on our lives is undeniable. We acknowledged the flaws of popular racism discourse and set the tone and pace for a journey of renewing our minds. To move forward, we must indeed move forward differently. Instead, we gained a solid foundation for what will be a life-long journey of deconstructing racism. Racism is like gravity, in that most of us know about it, but cannot explain how it works. Most people don't know the laws of physics that make gravity happen. Likewise, we see and talk about the evidence and outcomes of racism. for example, segregated churches, communities, and schools, opportunity gaps, and the prison industrial complex but lack an understanding of how it all

[139]

manifested the ideologies, the "science," the economic incentives, the social engineering, and the belief systems and laws that created it and hold it in place.

We learned what most of us do not know about racism but need to understand to create change and continued to build on that foundation by expanding our analysis of racism. With these, it helped us to examine how representations and stereotypes have shaped and informed our consciousness and decision making. We took a critical look at how policies created to serve some, have disadvantaged others. This encourages us to put feet to our prayers to actively and intentionally create change.

This offers this paradox: Racism was created by our country's founders. It is unfortunate that at a point in our nation's history, leaders deemed race/ism necessary for the success of our country. However, to know that race/ism was created by men driven by self-interests, means that like any man-made kingdom, it can fall. We can dismantle racism and create a more beautiful world.

We don't have to be defeated and determined by the lie, ideology, and legacy of race. We have been endowed by the

[140]

Creator with the creative power to over-throw this destroyer of souls and lives.

We can renew our minds, be curious about everything, no longer passively accept misinformation that deprives people and embrace the responsibility to be aware of the lies we've believed and inherited.

It's on us to choose a frame of oneness, grace, love, friendship, mercy, forgiveness, and justice. And within that frame, we can write journals or narratives that speak to the goodness in all of us. We actually can now live and "be" very different than before. But we have to intentionally reach for it!

"What do I do?" The race topic and conversation can be treacherous waters to navigate. So, we have designed to help equip, empower, and inspire you on your journey to becoming a viable part of healing for yourself and others.